ADAM and
DAVID a

MAKING YOUR HOME A HOLY PLACE

ASCENSION

West Chester, PA

Excerpts from the English translation of the *Catechism of the Catholic Church* for use in the United States of America © 1994 United States Catholic Conference, Inc.–Libreria Editrice Vaticana. Used with permission. English translation of the *Catechism of the Catholic Church: Modifications from the Editio Typica* © 1997 United States Conference of Catholic Bishops–Libreria Editrice Vaticana.

Unless otherwise noted, Scripture passages are from the Revised Standard Version–Second Catholic Edition © 2006 by the Division of Christian Education of the National Council of the Churches of Christ in the United States of America. Used by permission. All rights reserved.

Ascension
PO Box 1990
West Chester, PA 19380
1-800-376-0520
ascensionpress.com

The contents of this book were edited from articles and are used with kind permission of the Diocese of Tulsa and Eastern Oklahoma.

Cover design: Rosemary Strohm

Printed in the United States of America
22 23 24 25 26 5 4 3 2 1

ISBN 978-1-954881-38-9 (paperback)
ISBN 978-1-954881-39-6 (e-book)

CONTENTS

FOREWORD

When a man discerns a vocation to the priesthood, it is not unusual for someone to ask him, "Why do you want to be a priest?" Behind this question is an assumption that there must be some spiritual practices or a special call that led to this vocation.

In my experience, it is less common for a newly engaged couple to be asked the similar question, "Why do you want to get married?" Perhaps this is because there is an assumption that marriage is not rooted in spiritual practices or a special call akin to priesthood and religious life. But this is simply untrue. Marriage quite literally has as its purpose the building up of Christian society and culture, spirituality and cause. To the degree that husbands and wives are successful in building this society in their family, to that degree the larger society and the Church will be rich and life-giving.

This is why I love Living Beyond Sunday: Making Your Home a Holy Place. The purpose and holiness of marriage and family life are rooted in theology, philosophy, and an authentic human anthropology, but they must become incarnate in the nitty-gritty of the daily life of husbands and wives and their children, jobs, laundry, bath times, leisure time together, and prayer. The authors, David and Pamela, and Adam and Haylee, have done a fine job of taking the Church's wisdom about marriage and applying it to the everyday life of the family. While every family is different, this book will help all families renew and deepen the purpose for which the Lord brought them together and assist them as they seek to build their domestic church. May the Holy Family pray for all who read this book!

—Most Reverend David A. Konderla
Bishop of Tulsa and Eastern Oklahoma
Member of the Committee on Laity, Marriage,
Family Life, and Youth for the USCCB

INTRODUCTION

The family is mankind's oldest institution, going back to the very beginning when God commanded Adam and Eve to "be fruitful and multiply" (Genesis 1:28). The family, then, is the foundation of God's original plan for humanity. Man and woman have been created to form a lifelong, life-giving community to help one another—and their children—pursue holiness. Through their daily marital commitment, with all of its joys and challenges, a husband and a wife learn how to love and become more like God. Because the family is where we first learn about God and how to make an offering of our lives to him, we can truly call it a "domestic church."

The family home—our domestic church—should be a place of worship. At first glance, this may seem a strange concept. We don't typically connect our home and family life with Mass on Sunday. But the essence of our home life is meant to deepen our relationship with God and one another. For married couples, loving one's spouse is the primary way we are called to love and serve God. Therefore, when we do the dishes, set the table, or take out the trash—that is, when we do the ordinary, everyday things of domestic life—out of love, these small actions become acts of worship.

In the Gospels, we see many seeming paradoxes proclaimed: small things become big things, the least shall become the greatest, and the last shall be first. We often think of the saints as those few who did great things, such as St. Peter the Apostle or St. Joan of Arc, but what made them saints was their heroic sanctity and their love of Jesus in and above all things, not their achievements. Recall saints such as St. Thérèse of Lisieux and her "little way" and St. Teresa of Calcutta (Mother Teresa), performing small acts with great love. In our homes, then, learning to do small things with great love can make all the difference in our family's growth in holiness.

We wrote this short book to honor the "little things"—to bring glory to the ordinary, everyday acts of domestic life. In the following pages, we will frequently present an ideal vision for the domestic church. We are aware, though, that there can be a huge gap between this ideal and what happens in real life. Nonetheless, all of us are called to make our domestic church places where love of God and one another deepens every day. The thoughts shared in this book come from our own experience as husbands, wives, fathers, and mothers, as well as from the wisdom of the Church. We sincerely pray that you will find some insights here that will help you build and strengthen your own domestic church.

1

BUILDING THE
DOMESTIC CHURCH

The phrase "domestic church" is one that has become common in recent decades in the Church. It has its origin in the Second Vatican Council (1962–1965), and it is used prominently in its dogmatic constitution on the Church, *Lumen Gentium*. As the Council fathers write, "The family is, so to speak, the domestic church. In it parents should, by their word and example, be the first preachers of the faith to their children."[1]

This means that the home of a Catholic family needs to be a reflection of the universal Church—spiritually, emotionally, and relationally. When we think about it, we live the majority of our faith outside of "church," in our homes and with our families. If we want to live a truly authentic Christian life, wouldn't it make sense to make our homes like a "church away from church"?

While a growing number of families today are homeschooling, most children continue to receive their formal education outside of the home. Yet the home will always be where they—and the family as a whole—are truly formed at the deepest level. It is in the lessons of home life where they learn the value of virtue and the virulence of vice. It is through the domestic routine that faith is either reinforced by habitual prayer and devotion—or is left impoverished as merely a weekly obligation to attend Mass. While education can form our minds, then the home—the domestic church—is where we form our hearts. For all these reasons, we should strive to make our home a sanctuary from temptation, consumerism, and relativism.

In a 1979 homily during his pastoral visit to the United States, St. John Paul II summed up perfectly the responsibilities within families by stating, "To maintain a joyful family requires much from both the parents and children. Each member of the family has to become, in a special way, the servant of the others."[2] We need to see how we can truly serve one another in love every day, parent to parent, parent to child, and siblings to one another.

We can start "building our domestic church" in simple ways, such as by placing religious art throughout our homes, praying before meals, and striving to treat each other with patience and kindness. We can then move on to some things that require more effort, such as praying the Rosary or the Liturgy of the Hours as a family. Experience has shown that the more effort something takes, the greater the impact it will have on our families.

Adam: Growing up, my parents would gather us into the living room every night to read a passage from the Bible and pray the Rosary together. This had such a powerful impact in helping form us in our devotional life as a family. As Catholics, we are called to live our faith *outside* of our parish churches, apart from attending Mass on Sunday. We are called to live our faith in our everyday lives, particularly within our homes.

The domestic church is intended to be a "saint-making machine." If a husband and wife take every opportunity to sacrifice for one another, fast for one another, and express love and affection toward each other, then ultimately they will help the other attain holiness and reach closer to the heavenly reward. Jesus perfectly exemplified this for his Church by laying down his life for her, and marriage is an image of this sacrificial love (see Ephesians 5:32), where spouses lay down their lives for one another. In turn, this shared sacrificial love between a husband and wife can bring about new life—growing their domestic church and the universal Church.

In the Gospel of John, Jesus gives us the beautiful image of the vines and the branches, saying, "I am the vine, you are the branches. He who abides in me, and I in him, he it is that bears much fruit, for apart from me you can do nothing" (John 15:5). In our domestic church, we can work together in the Lord to bear the best fruit. Jesus goes on to say, "These things I have spoken to you, that my joy may be in you, and that your joy may be full" (John 15:11). May we truly hold Jesus as the joy of all our desires and find in him the strength to live fully alive.

Of course, we must have realistic expectations for our family, understanding that each family's dynamic is unique. At the same time, we need to maintain a firm grip on the end goal: a family filled with the joy and love of Jesus Christ. As parents, we must reflect on ways we are revealing and communicating the joy and love of God in our homes so we can rightly and boldly say, "As for me and my house, we will serve the LORD" (Joshua 24:15).

2

MARRIAGE: THE HEART OF THE DOMESTIC CHURCH

As we continue our consideration of the domestic church, it is fitting to start at the beginning. Marriage is the heart and foundation of the domestic church and is the fuel that feeds the furnace of love in the home. If a home is inhabited by a loving marriage, there is a warm joy that envelops it. Even in times of sorrow, this joy can be felt, becoming a background to what would otherwise be moments of sadness. As the Second Vatican Council expresses, "The well-being of the individual person and of both human and Christian society is closely bound up with the healthy state of conjugal and family life."[3]

An interesting occurrence takes place in a home when a wood stove or fireplace is lit. The whole family crowds into one room to be near its warmth, almost in celebration of this miracle of heat. Bright, enticing, and warm, all are drawn to experience the fire. However, if not tended to diligently, the fire will start to die, and so too the invisible bonds of proximity that served to unite the family around it. It is the same with marriage—the greater the love between the spouses, the greater the unity of the family.

A loving marriage, then, draws in the entire family, warming hearts as a fire warms the cheeks of those mesmerized in its flame. If there is no total self-gift between a husband and wife, though, the flame will slowly die, and the home will grow cold. Only a holy marriage bears an assortment of fruits; it will be more colorful and brilliant than all the flowers of the field. However, the soil in which these fruits and flowers grow is the love between spouses.

The theme of marriage permeates all of Scripture, beginning with the creation of Adam and Eve and ending with the wedding feast of the Lamb in the book of Revelation (see CCC 1602). God continually draws our attention back to the fidelity and love that is the cornerstone of holy Matrimony. Ultimately, a beautiful domestic church cannot be built on anything other than a loving marriage. As the *Catechism of the Catholic Church* notes, "The example and teaching given by parents and families remain the special form of [marriage] preparation" (CCC 1632). Better marriages beget better domestic churches—which in turn beget a new generation of better marriages and better domestic churches.

The very first instruction God gives to man in the Bible is "be fruitful and multiply" (Genesis 1:28). Marriage, then, is fundamental to the divine plan. In Genesis, we see God create humanity in his own image, and this divine imitation is fully expressed in the union of man and woman. What a blessed privilege we have in being created in the image of God! The dignity we possess because of this allows us to be capable of self-knowledge, self-possession, and therefore self-gift (CCC 357). The man freely, totally, faithfully, and fruitfully gives his love to his bride; she receives it and gives it back freely, totally, faithfully, and fruitfully to her husband. Through this gift, man and woman reflect the Father's work of creation (CCC 2205).

As the fathers of Vatican II tell us, "It is imperative to give suitable and timely instruction to young people, above all in the heart of their own families, about the dignity of married love, its role and its exercise, so that, having learned the value of chastity, they will be able at a suitable age to engage in honorable courtship and enter upon a marriage of their own."[4] The domestic church is the first place where our children will come to know the love of God.

The common wisdom is that parents are called always to put their children first, but this is not true. Our faith teaches us that the relationship between spouses is the most important relationship to be fueled in the home.

Children are the *fruit* of the vocation of marriage; the
relationship between spouses is the foundation of the
vocation itself. While we as parents have an obligation to
our children to tend the fire of our love, we have a primary
obligation to our spouse. *Pamela:* In the wise words of my
father, Dan O'Brien, "I *chose* your mother; you kids just
showed up later."

The greatest gift parents can give their children is to
love one another. If spouses are not prioritizing their
relationship above all others, they are doing a disservice
not only to themselves and their children, but to the entire
community as well. Children deserve a home in which
their parents' love for one another reigns supreme so that
they can grow up in a secure, loving environment. Examine
your marriage—what does it look like from your children's
perspective? What do you do to obviously show love to
your spouse in front of your children?

Here are some examples that can easily be incorporated
into daily life which help cultivate love between husband
and wife:

1. **Never speak poorly of your spouse to
   anyone.** It can be easy to fall into the trap of
   complaining about your spouse, especially
   if present company is all doing the same.

But the truth is that this is a severe breach of the vows you made at the altar: "I will love you and *honor* you all the days of my life" (without the qualification "... unless my friends or coworkers are throwing their spouses under the bus, in which case I reserve the right to do the same to you"). It is our sacred task to uphold the dignity of our spouse in our words and actions. Let us in all things imitate Christ who seeks to present his bride the Church "in splendor, without spot or wrinkle or any such thing, that she might be holy and without blemish" (Ephesians 5:27).

2. **When you arrive home, seek to greet your spouse *before* greeting your children.** It can be difficult to ignore the floodgates breaking loose as your children scream, "Daddy's home!" and rush to greet you at the door (and in all honesty, few moments in life are as precious as these). But there is a lesson to be learned, subtle and profound, when the first words out of a father's mouth after hugging his children are, "Where is your mother?" Before he asks them how their day was or listens to the story they have been so eagerly waiting to tell, reverence must first be paid to his beloved bride. This is yet another

reminder to your children that the priority of your spousal relationship is why the furnace of love burns fiercely in your home.

3. **Pray for your spouse out loud, in front of your children.** While you may pray for your spouse at various times throughout the day for various intentions, specific or general, it is imperative that your children know you do so. This is not to say that the children must know your spouse's wounds or weaknesses in detail; some issues should remain between parents. That said, each family member should be tending to one another's spiritual as well as physical needs, and parents should take the lead. For example, at our house, we always add to the end of the meal prayer, "God bless Dad" when David is absent from our meal. Our children know without a doubt that Dad and Mom pray for each other.

4. **Never allow your children to speak disrespectfully to you or your spouse.** You are the guardians of your spouse's dignity, and it is your job to make sure he or she is honored and respected, especially in your home. "Yes, sir" and "yes, ma'am" show that a culture of respect and dignity is upheld within the family.

Polite manners easily curtail, and then the habit vanishes; they must be preserved and protected for the good of the whole family.

5. **Fast regularly for your spouse.** If the sacrament of Matrimony calls us to our fullest expression of love, then we must learn to lay down our lives in order to love in the way God is calling us to love. "Greater love has no man than this, that a man lay down his life for his friends" (John 15:13). Most of us will not receive the grace of physical martyrdom. However, this does not mean that God is not calling each of us to die to self in small ways for the good of our family, including fasting. Husbands should consider fasting for their wife at least once a month. Men from all over the world participate in a bread and water fast on the first Wednesday of every month (see our Recommended Resources at the back of this book for more information on this). Wives, too, should be offering up intentional prayers and fasting for the sanctity of their husband. Specifically praying for Dad during family prayers, when he is absent, offering the monotonies of the day for his sanctification, and making dietary sacrifices are all examples of how

to continue to learn to die to self for the good of the other. Becoming one flesh is a great mystery, even to St. Paul, who says, "Let each one of you love his wife as himself, and let the wife see that she respects her husband" (Ephesians 5:33).

6. **Date nights.** Spending time together as spouses, away from the kids, is necessary to strengthen your relationship. Date nights will look different to every couple and will vary in frequency across the different seasons in your marriage.

Ultimately, only bountiful marriages can transform our domestic churches into sanctuaries for this liturgy of love; and it is this liturgy by which we sanctify our daily lives and the world.

Prayer of Married Persons to St. Joachim and St. Anne[5]

O models of pious and virtuous married persons, St. Joachim and St. Anne! Through the wondrous blessing with which God gladdened your hearts when he chose you as the parents of the ever blessed Virgin, the mother of Our Savior, obtain for us, we beseech you, the grace to desire nothing but virtue and piety; that, in fidelity and love, we may share each other's joys and sorrows and together with our children lead such a life as to insure our entrance into the kingdom of heaven! Amen.

3

FATHERHOOD AND THE DOMESTIC CHURCH

Fatherhood is the greatest, most noble calling of a man. What an incredible honor that, as fathers, through the grace of Christ, we are called to reflect the fatherhood of God to our families. As St. Paul writes, "For this reason I bow my knees before the Father, from whom every family in heaven and on earth is named" (see Ephesians 3:14–15). Our families, then, have their very foundation in God the Father—so we, as fathers, have an awesome responsibility.

As St. John Paul II has said, "As the family goes, so goes the nation, and so goes the whole world in which we live." Building on these powerful words, we can confidently say, "as fatherhood goes, so goes the family." A father stands at the head of his household, and it is his example and direction that make a family strong—or weak. While this is often a contentious point in our modern times, the proper role of fathers needs to be restored if we want to revitalize our families, our nation, and our world.

But what exactly *is* fatherhood?

God the Father has fashioned human fatherhood after his own, so a father might be a symbol of our heavenly Father within his domestic church. Not only do fathers have spiritual authority over their families, but the authority of God is stamped into their very bodies. It is to men that God has given the ability to author new life. As a sign of his power, God imbued his might into the muscles of men and placed them as guardians over the family.

To better understand what fatherhood *is*, let's take a look at what a father *does*. The basic obligations of fatherhood are threefold: to *protect*, *provide*, and *establish*. (While this analysis is primarily focused on fatherhood in a family, a single man can apply these principles to those souls God has placed within his care and influence.)

1. **Protect.** Thankfully, gone are the days when a father would worry about wild animals attacking his family in the night (at least in most countries!). But our modern conveniences and luxuries have a way of blinding us to the necessity of vigilance.

The frontiersman who led his family through the wilderness knew he needed to be watchful and prepared for whatever he encountered. Today, it takes more than a rifle and sturdy shelter to safeguard our families. The beasts that prowl these days are not easily defeated. We do not face the mountain lion or the bear, but secularism, consumerism, violence, and pornography ... and these modern evils are far more malevolent than a wild bear or lion: "Do not fear those who kill the body but cannot kill the soul; rather fear him who can destroy both soul and body in hell" (Matthew 10:28).

These days, we need to be on guard against the technology we use every day. If we as fathers are not doing whatever we can to ensure that our kids' devices—their smartphones, laptops, tablets, etc.—are "locked down" and content restricted, we are failing in our duty. Make sure you set limits on how much time they spend online—and monitor what they are doing and where they are going. (There are many programs you can install to filter and monitor your children's devices. For a few suggestions, please see the Recommended Resources section at the back of this book.)

No matter how virtuous your child may be, the world—in all its pornography, violence, and profanity—is pursuing your children through the Internet, anxiously waiting for a moment of curiosity to poison and enslave their souls. The bottom line: Just as you would defend your children from a lion or other predator, it is your job to protect them from the dangerous predators that lurk online.

2. **Provide.** As St. Paul makes clear, a Christian father should accept his responsibility to be a provider: "If any one does not provide for his relatives, and especially for his own family, he has disowned the faith and is worse than an unbeliever" (1 Timothy 5:8). Simply providing an income for the family does not fulfill this obligation. Being a provider requires our *time*, *talent*, and *treasure* in more than just a material sense.

   Time. At home, we need to give time to the spiritual and physical needs of our wife and children—and we cannot do this if we are distracted. In the *Screwtape Letters*, C.S. Lewis describes a senior-level demon named Screwtape teaching a junior tempter how to distract Christians from relationships that matter most in life. Screwtape tells his student to get his subject to do nothing at all for long periods of time through meaningless distractions.

How much of our time is spent doing nothing while hypnotized by a screen, procrastinating fulfilling our responsibilities? The world offers plenty of meaningless distractions that keep us from our relationship with God and family. To combat this, we must be intentional and unwavering in developing traditions in the home that cultivate quality family time. We need to ask ourselves, *Are we going to be consumers or producers when we get home from work? Will our kids see us as dads who generate fun, games, prayer, and memories? Or are they constantly begging for our attention as we are watching TV, checking email, or distracted online?*

We need to be intentional and guard the time we have to grow together as a family. While spending quality time with our children is extremely important, we must remember who's, not what's, our first vocation. We cannot neglect spending quality time with our wife. Eating meals at the dinner table, praying as a family, having family game nights, or setting up a tent for a backyard camping night all facilitate important moments to have meaningful and worthwhile conversations that will forge the family bond.

Talent. To fulfill the admonition of St. Peter to "employ [our gifts] for one another" (1 Peter 4:10), we must utilize our God-given talents in service to our family so that it may flourish. One of the many things these authors will be ashamed of at our judgment is when God shows us all the graces and talents he gave us for the betterment of our families that were completely wasted due to pride or apathy. We have a duty to attend to the sanctification of our family, and we must trust that God has given us all we need to raise our children to be good Christians, productive citizens, and saints for heaven. Our sons will be paying attention to see how we pray, handle adversity, and pursue virtue. Our daughters will look to see how we love our wife, show compassion to those in need, and protect the vulnerable. As fathers, we must do all we can to provide for our families. In doing so, we seek to provide them with the best God has given to us.

Treasure. St. Thomas Aquinas, citing Cicero, shares that the virtue of temperance gives order and balance in our life.[6] Temperance is important in terms of our treasure. By exercising this virtue, we can incorporate a family financial plan to avoid unnecessary debt, increase deliberate tithing, and moderate consumerism. How can we teach our children to be good stewards of our treasure? We must first instill gratitude for the things we have. This can be as simple as starting evening prayer with, "God, we come to you as a family in thanksgiving for all the many blessings, gifts, and graces you have bestowed on us today. Forgive us when we have failed to use those gifts in accordance with your will." If we aren't thankful for the gifts God has given, we will be discontented with what we receive. Encourage them to work hard to achieve their goals. When they run into adversity, offer them the guidance they need to persevere. Counsel them to share the blessings they have been given with others.

3. **Establish.** The duty of fatherhood reaches its crescendo in our charge to establish our children in the true, the good, and the beautiful. In fact, our duty to *protect* and *provide* points to our

authority and obligation to *establish*. Why defend
our children's innocence if we are not going to
teach them modesty and chastity? Why provide
them the necessities of life if we do not teach
them to one day stand on their own? If we
divorce our fatherhood from our ultimate goal
of training our children in the ways of sanctity,
then the burdens of "protecting" and "providing"
become just that, burdens. Is it any wonder
why our culture has adopted this burdensome
attitude toward large families?

In his song "Easy Like Sunday Morning," it is likely that
singer Lionel Richie was not referencing parents getting
their children ready for church. In most families, Sunday
mornings are filled with controlled chaos as they strive to
get everyone dressed and prepared for the most important
event of the entire week—Sunday Mass.

Adam: One Sunday, walking out the door to church, I
noticed my son had a Lego man in his hand. Quickly, I told
him we don't bring Legos to Mass and to go put it back up
in his room. It wasn't until halfway through the homily that
I looked over to see him holding a dinosaur figurine. "Bud,
what did I tell you?" I asked in the church parking lot after
Mass. "You said no Legos. I brought a dinosaur," he replied.
I let a half-smile escape, impressed my son was creative

enough to obey what was asked yet found a loophole to still get what he wanted.

Similarly, we can think of instances in our faith life where we try to obey the Lord while constantly looking for a loophole to keep doing our will. If we are following the Church's teachings out of obligation or fear, then we really aren't doing it out of love. Instead of pursuing heaven, we often focus on avoiding hell. We need to teach our children to pursue the good, not simply avoid the bad. If we simply lay down the rules in our homes without giving the reason for them, this fails to provide them with the understanding needed to form their appetites to choose the good willingly. We must seek to guide them and help them desire the true, the good, and the beautiful in their lives.

God the Father gave us commandments to make us holy, not to be a tyrant. Similarly, we must exercise our authority in our homes, not as tyrants, but as gentle and loving fathers who help form the intellects and wills of our children to pursue virtue and avoid vice. For the authority Christ gives to us is never for our own gain but for the gain of those who are entrusted to us. St. Paul calls husbands to love their wives as Jesus loved the Church—by laying down his life for her (see Ephesians 5:25). It is a self-sacrificial, complete giving of oneself for the good of the other. It is the Cross. God wills it, nature imposes it, and our salvation depends on it. Hopefully, as our children grow and face tough decisions in life, their conscience and appetites will be formed to look, not for the loopholes, but for the will of our heavenly Father.

Prayer for Fathers

O God, to how many great temptations of body and soul are my children exposed! How insufficient is the protection I can give them. Yes, Lord, "In vain, I watch over them if you do not assist me." But if they dwell "in the aid of the Most High, and abide under the protection of the God of Jacob," how contented may I not be! Receive them, O Lord, my children, under your protection. Keep them far from all dangers of soul and body; give them health. But above all protect them from danger to their souls. Keep far from them all that may exercise a hurtful influence on their young hearts and become an occasion of sin to them. Preserve them from sin. Send "your holy angels to keep them in all their ways that they may bear them up in their hands, lest they dash their feet against a stone." O almighty God and Father, lead my children through the dangers and storms of this life, that they may enter safely into the haven of salvation. Amen.

4

MOTHERHOOD AND THE DOMESTIC CHURCH

Take a moment to meditate upon the following mothers: Our Mother Mary, weeping at the foot of the Cross. Imagine her cousin Elizabeth or Sarah, Abraham's wife, going through pregnancy and mothering a toddler at such advanced ages! Then we see Ruth's great devotion to her mother-in-law at the expense of leaving behind the world she knew. Don't forget Jochebed, who placed her beloved son, Moses, in a basket in a river in order that he not be killed by the Egyptians. While the trials for these mothers are pronounced, the joy of their motherhood is so much greater. Love is a choice, though sometimes not a pretty one. Motherhood looks different with each woman, each family; however, there is one unifying thread that we can all agree upon—love.

Love is a great act of service. Jesus constantly reminds us that he is the "servant of the Lord" and that he came "not to be served but to serve" (Mark 10:45). In true discipleship, Mary imitates her son and unites her will with the will of our heavenly Father. In her *fiat*, Mary expresses that she is the "handmaid of the Lord" (Luke 1:38).

As St. John Paul II notes in his encyclical *Mulieris Dignitatem* ("On the Dignity and Vocation of Women"), to serve means to reign.[7] The vocation of a mother, and of all women, is to serve, to love. Women have a place in the kingdom that we can attain if we are animated with the love of Christ! We have been crowned with God's glory and are able to give him the highest praise and honor by using our unique gifts as women. Entrusted with these particular gifts, we can more easily labor diligently and beautifully, knowing that it is for the greater glory of God through our vocation, not just fulfilling secular domestic duty.

TWO PARTICULAR CALLINGS

Mary encompasses perfectly two of the "particular dimensions of the female personality," of which St. John Paul II speaks—motherhood and virginity. These dimensions co-exist in the person of the Mother of God, which "helps everyone—especially women—to see how these two dimensions, these two paths in the vocation of women as persons, explain and complete each other."[8] These gifts are fully received by Mary at her *fiat*. She appreciates both of these gifts and responds generously and wholly to them. Practically speaking, children tend to decrease availability to respond generously to the (often urgent or last-minute) needs of others. However, Mary demonstrates that availability resides in a disposition of receptivity, a practice of putting oneself aside and making room for the other. And so a woman can and should manifest these two complementary dimensions as she receives, appreciates, and responds with readiness and faith to the gifts God has bestowed upon her.

Christ, the Bridegroom, seeks to give his bride, the Church, an example of holy motherhood. "Motherhood is the fruit of the marriage union of a man and woman" and expresses itself in two becoming one flesh.[9] Mary is perfectly the spouse of the Holy Spirit and carries the flesh of our Savior in her womb. Married women are called to be devoted to their husbands in a physical and real way— by becoming a total gift of self and participating in the spousal union, and by being devoted to Christ through our participation in the Church, the Bride of Christ, "without spot or wrinkle" (Ephesians 5:27). As a bride, we can cultivate the gift of interior readiness to receive and therefore give.

An invaluable gift we have as a bride is to be present. It can be very easy to submerge ourselves in the "busyness" culture that surrounds us. After all, many women are juggling several roles—wife, mother, employee, parishioner, and volunteer, just to name a few. Setting clear boundaries of what takes precedence is crucial to giving our gifts to the fullest. This time cannot be recaptured. If our hearts are set on furthering the kingdom of God, we should certainly prioritize the time we have with our families in prayer and nurturing. As one wife and mother once said, "Never once have I regretted saying 'no' and staying home." We need to give our husbands and families not only the gift of our physical presence but also our mental and spiritual presence.

In this light, let's consider the family table. Studies have shown that regularly sharing meals is a substantial contributing factor to the well-being of families. We are able to fully connect with our family members, and be present to them, through the breaking of bread, enjoying the fruits of our labor, and appreciating the thoughtfulness and detail of how the meal comes together. As Bishop Thomas Olmsted of the Diocese of Phoenix writes in his pastoral letter *Complete My Joy*, "Satan is committed to filling up our lives with other things to do. The more busy we make ourselves in giving in to this temptation, the more difficult it will be to sit down to eat as a family."[10]

The family meal is a beautiful and fulfilling way women are able to give the gift of their total selves in an act of service. St. John Paul II emboldens us to search and, in the words of Vatican II, "fully find [ourselves] through "a sincere gift of [ourselves]."[11]

SUFFERING AND MOTHERHOOD

With our unique, God-given feminine gifts come certain sufferings. Again, these look different for each woman. Certainly each woman has an idea of what her sufferings entail, whether they be physical, mental, emotional, and/or spiritual.

As we consider the example of the Blessed Mother kneeling in sorrow at the foot of her Son's cross, so too we, as Christian mothers, should give ourselves up completely to God's holy will. Mary has much to teach us, as we ponder her Seven Sorrows along with our own motherhood.

1. ***The Prophecy of St. Simeon:*** Do I reflect upon the gift, the child, with which God has entrusted me? This is firstly God's child. God has a particular plan for this child. May I receive this plan with receptivity and grace, knowing that at times I will be disappointed or hurt.

2. ***The Escape and Flight into Egypt:*** Help me to
   accept the suffering inflicted upon me. Help me
   to keep my child safe from all harm, particularly
   from sins against innocence and purity.

3. ***The Loss of the Child Jesus in the Temple
   of Jerusalem:*** The experience of loss is a
   disorienting one. Do I rely on myself in these
   moments of suffering, or do I trust in the Lord's
   goodness? As the psalmist says of the righteous
   person, "He is not afraid of evil tidings; his heart
   is firm, trusting in the LORD" (Psalm 112:7).

4. ***The Meeting of Mary and Jesus on the Via
   Dolorosa:*** As a mother, my children need me to
   be there for them. Am I doing my best to put to
   death the things in my life that are preventing me
   from being fully present to my children?

5. ***The Crucifixion of Jesus on Mount Calvary:***
   As St. Ignatius of Loyola prayed, "Teach [me]
   to give and not count the cost." Do I love,
   serve, and care for my family with a cheerful
   and giving disposition? For this is my vocation
   as wife and mother.

6. ***The Piercing of the Side of Jesus and His Descent from the Cross:*** Do I recognize the importance of the most precious Blood of Jesus? Help me to prioritize Holy Mass and the sacraments in my life.

7. ***The Burial of Jesus:*** As the tomb is closed, Lord, open my heart to your grace. Be with me always as I contemplate how your suffering and death lead us to eternal life with you. Help me to comfort my children when they are tempted to despair by reminding them of the great mercy of God.

As Fr. Shannon Collins of the Missionaries of St. John the Baptist beautifully states, "The tears shed by many mothers are a mystery. A mystery that will further serve to water the tree of the cross, producing ever-more abundant fruits of redemption."[12] When we freely give of ourselves through suffering, we are choosing to glorify God no matter the circumstances, whether it be doing our regular domestic duties without any recognition from those we love or watching our children make devastating mistakes in which our only response can be prayer. Whatever the case may be, our heart has much to suffer.

Think of dear St. Monica and her trials. She endured an awful family dynamic with an adulterous husband and a wayward son, St. Augustine. Through her constant prayer, fasting, and undoubtedly tears, God used these sufferings to further sanctify her and, eventually, her husband and son too. The sorrow we withstand for the good of our family is sanctifying if we welcome the transformation God has willed for us.

Maintaining peace during suffering will be difficult. God will always provide his presence and his peace, which will fulfill our lives according to his Divine will, according to the cross he asks us to bear. Be mindful of your loved ones' sufferings also. Above all, be grateful for one another's gifts and dignity as a member of your family.

RAISING OUR CHILDREN

In raising his little ones, we must rely on God's grace and the authority he has given us as mothers. Jesus' first miracle at the wedding at Cana showcases a prime example of our Blessed Mother exercising her authority. Jesus dutifully obeys his mother by honoring her request of turning water into wine. Just as Mary led her Son to perform this miracle, so we have the obligation to lead our children to fulfill and obey what God has set in his natural and divine laws. Practically, this could mean forming their conscience through discipline, encouraging almsgiving and sacrifice, or quite literally, any instance that would further the kingdom of God.

If, as parents, and specifically mothers, we have "a completely original and irreplaceable role in raising children," then we need to really step up and get serious about correctly and lovingly forming the souls who have been entrusted to us.[13] It is our responsibility to teach them to love the true, the good, and the beautiful. We should strive to uphold virtue in our households through modest dress, respectful conversations, and sacramental living, as "the home is well suited for education in the virtues" (CCC 2223). A gift of true freedom, to our children and to ourselves for that matter, can only be given through solid lessons in self-denial, sound judgment, and self-mastery (see CCC 2223). If we do not do this as mothers, who will?

A mother must be watchful for any vices that may sneak into her children's behavior. If lying becomes an issue, as it almost inevitably will with children, she must not only consistently forbid untruths to be told, regardless of the time it will take to correct the child, but also promote the good and reward the children when they are honest. She must always be guarding her children to defend the purity and innocence that justice is due to them. This may be done through vigilance and prayer. Do not wait until bad habits have taken hold. As the book of Proverbs tells us, "Train up a child in the way he should go, and when he is old he will not depart from it" (Proverbs 22:6).

FOSTERING A LOVING HOME

Women, by their nature, have a remarkable ability to see the whole human being as an irreplaceable gift from God. As St. Teresa Benedicta of the Cross (Edith Stein) writes, "Woman naturally seeks to embrace that which is living, personal, and whole. To cherish, guard, protect, nourish, and advance growth is her natural, maternal yearning."[14] It is this ability that gives them the perfect heart to guard, nurture, and protect the family that has been entrusted to them. Wives and mothers are the calm of the storm, the refuge during chaos, the ones who can quiet a wild soul. "As one whom his mother comforts, so I will comfort you" (Isaiah 66:13).

The mother ought to go to great lengths to give her husband and each of her children a sense of belonging to the family. Loving obviously means giving of yourself, but it also means forgiving others. Teach your children to forgive one another; show forgiveness yourself when someone has wronged you. A lot of meaning comes from these little words. When a family can be confident in one another's mercy toward them, love and trust can truly bloom.

One of the greatest joys a woman can receive is that of gratitude from her husband. When he returns home from the tumultuous outside world and is welcomed by a warm and peaceful home, she can be assured that her service of love has not been in vain. The work and sacrifices performed by a wife and mother, when done with love, will yield a strong and harmonious family dynamic. Just as a husband and father is obligated to protect and provide for his family, so too the wife has an obligation to stand in love and fear of God, to be courageous, and to be the heart in her home.

Prayer of Mothers for their Children[15]

*Good and gracious God, we thank you, that you
have given us children, made them heirs of heaven
by holy baptism, and entrusted to us their training.
Fill us with a sense of our responsibility; assist us
in the care of their health, but especially in the
preservation of their innocence and purity of heart.
Grant that we may teach them early to know and
serve you, and to love you, with their whole heart.
Grant that we ourselves may carefully avoid all that
we must forbid them, and may assiduously practice
all that we should teach them. We commend
them, O God, to your paternal care and to the
guardianship of your holy angels. Bless our efforts,
O heavenly Father, and let our children develop
to your honor and persevere in virtue till the end.
Amen.*

5

LIVING LITURGICALLY IN THE DOMESTIC CHURCH

What does the phrase "living liturgically" mean anyway? If the home can truly be called a domestic church, does this mean there is a corresponding liturgy to be celebrated in the residential sanctuary? Yes, it most certainly does! This household liturgy, of course, is not as formal or as structured as what we find in the Roman Missal. For example, there is no official book of "general instructions" offering us as celebrants of our domestic liturgies instructions to "do this" and "say that." (Wouldn't it be nice if there was?) Nonetheless, there is a way of living liturgically within the home that can bring your domestic church into step with the life and rhythm of the universal Church.

Does this mean we should wear "vestment-shaped ponchos" around the house and say things such as "it is right and just" after someone thanks you for passing the green beans at the dinner table? As interesting (and a bit odd) as such things might be, they would miss the mark. Living liturgically does not involve trying to "do the Mass" at home; rather, it is about allowing our home life to be informed and guided by the same "spirit" that informs and guides the official Liturgy of the Church.

THE IMPORTANCE OF THE LITURGICAL CALENDAR

The Church's liturgical calendar is full of feasts, fasts, and hope. The incarnation and resurrection of Jesus are the most significant events that ever took place on earth. They are so significant that it would seem reasonable to do nothing but celebrate Easter every day. If Christ is risen, why do we still go through Lent every year? Why do we have forty days of penance and fasting? Why are we not in jubilation every day that Christ is risen?

Well, the Church, in its wisdom, knows that we are not ready for this kind of "non-stop" jubilation. We need to prepare ourselves to celebrate it. In the gospel, Jesus gives us the parable of a wedding banquet where a man is driven out of the feast because he came without wearing the proper attire (see Matthew 22:11–14). In other words, he was unprepared to celebrate. Over the course of the liturgical year, we oscillate between feasting and fasting—

with the hope that, over the years, we learn to do each one a little better. In heaven, we will celebrate the Eternal Feast of the Lamb—that is, "Easter every day"—but as we walk with the Lord on earth, we need the liturgical seasons.

The great thing about living according to the liturgical calendar is that nearly every day is a feast. Whether we are visiting the homebound of our parish on the feast of the Visitation of Mary on May 31, baking a cake for Our Lady's birthday on September 8, grilling steak on the feast of St. Lawrence on August 10, having cinnamon rolls on the feast of St. Lucy on December 13, or eating a favorite dish on the feast of our patron saint, living our lives by the calendar of the Church has a way of transforming our homes into "a land flowing with milk and honey."

LIVING THE LITURGICAL SEASONS

There are six seasons in the liturgical calendar: Advent, Christmas, Lent, Triduum, Easter, and Ordinary Time. This yearly cycle blesses the faithful with the ability to participate more fully in the life and mystery of Christ. Be creative and bold in your celebrations! During Advent, be intentional when putting up that gorgeous Christmas tree. Gather the family, turn on your favorite Christmas carols, light a fire in the fireplace, and reminisce about your favorite family memories while each member of the family takes turns decorating the tree. Keep it up until January 12, when we celebrate the Baptism of the Lord. During Lent, decorate with barren burlap instead of cheery spring blossoms. One example that has been widely beneficial in the domestic church is to cover prominent holy images, specifically images of Jesus and the crucifix, during the two weeks leading up to Easter known as Passiontide. Then, on Easter, unveil these images to live anew with the Risen Lord.

Living liturgically in the home can reveal the profound truth that all things sing a beautiful hymn of life to our Creator. Within this "hymn of the home," each verse has a distinct place and beauty. Our homes have distinct places to gather for nourishment, recreation, and rest. But do we have a special place to gather for prayer and worship?

Just as in the sanctuary of a church, our home, too, needs a space in which its liturgical life can be rooted. Prepare a quiet yet prominent place in the home where everyone can come together and orient themselves to prayer. This could involve a small table or "altar" with a cloth draped over it to match the color of the liturgical season. Some blessed items you might want to add: a crucifix, either on the table or on the wall nearby; blessed candles; an image of the Blessed Virgin Mary (perhaps the Immaculate Heart) or the Sacred Heart of Jesus; and a small vase to place flowers as a beautiful offering to the Lord.

Place a Bible on the table. Begin each day with the daily Mass readings. (These can be found on the USCCB website or in a missalette.) They have been chosen wisely to harmonize the liturgy in accordance with the saint of the day or the specific liturgical season of the Church. Scripture unites our domestic church's hymn with that of the universal Church. Our sacred place should be the climactic verse within the song that defines the family and unites all the verses together to create a beautiful hymn. Encourage family members to spend time reading the Bible in this sacred space.

PRAYING AS A DOMESTIC CHURCH

Most of us have heard the famous quote attributed to Fr. Patrick Peyton, "The family that prays together stays together." Imagine if a poll were taken that asked, "Do you think your family would benefit from praying more together?" Most families would respond with a resounding yes. The follow-up question, "How are you going to increase your family prayer time?" is a bit tougher to answer. Adding "one more thing" into the family schedule sounds almost impossible for most families. However, instead of looking at "increasing family prayer time" as something we need to add in addition to our busy lives, perhaps we can look at it as something we integrate into what we are already doing within our daily lives.

At times, attempting to develop a family prayer routine with small children can seem more like a physical workout than a spiritual one. Quickly grabbing a runaway child, diffusing a wrestling match between siblings mid-prayer, or making sure a rosary isn't being wrapped around a little one's neck can leave you feeling exhausted or, worse, hopeless at the end of family prayer time. Rest assured that these trials are not unique to your family. They should be accepted with humor as much as possible. Take comfort knowing you are ardently striving for your family to pray together, which is pleasing to the Lord.

Involving your children and giving them individual tasks during prayer time brings an order, structure, and routine to family prayer that will eventually lead to a more peaceful and reverent atmosphere. For example, when you begin praying the Rosary together, make sure each child knows what will happen and how each will participate. One child can be in charge of gathering the rosaries and passing them out to each family member. Another can be in charge of lighting and blowing out the prayer candle (which usually creates a calm, reverent atmosphere as the kids are mesmerized by the flame). If you decide to use incense, an older child can be in charge of it. The more senses you can integrate into family prayer, the better.

By using a "wall rosary" in your family prayer, each child can easily take a turn praying a decade. For example, dad starts the prayer and prays the first decade using the wall rosary and then passes it to mom to lead the next decade. She then passes it to a child, who prays the next decade, and so on. For those blessed with big families, you can alternate which children pray the decades. This is a great way to orient the family to the sacred and into a deeper relationship with our Lord, all while instilling the importance of the family being united on the path toward holiness.

Given the chaos of daily life, it is helpful to have a structured prayer routine. Consider the liturgical season or the particular saint being commemorated each day. This can help the entire family learn about the Faith and develop specific prayer intentions and devotions. It is important not only *to* pray but also to be clear *for what* and *for whom* we are praying.

One way to do this is by implementing a "prayer board." The prayer board is a place in which each family member's name, prayer intention, and their choice of intercessory saint for their specific prayer is listed. For example, the board will show that "Gabriel" is praying for an increase in virtue through the intercession of St. Joseph. Repeat this process for every member of the family. An ideal spot to hang your family's board is a common gathering place, perhaps on a wall near the kitchen table. Discuss your prayer board every day, maybe during or after dinner. Come up with a family prayer and family saint. Together, pray for the intentions mentioned that evening. Throughout the next day, family members will have a visual reminder not only to pray but to pray for specific intentions. This practice can help establish regular prayer within your domestic church— and whoever else you welcome to your table!

Another devotional you may want to implement is praying the Liturgy of the Hours (LOH), also known as the Divine Office. The Liturgy of the Hours is the official liturgical prayer of the Church, prayed at specific times during the day. This practice was developed in the monasteries, and it is required to be prayed every day by bishops, priests, deacons, and the majority of consecrated religious. In recent decades, a growing number of laypeople have begun praying the Liturgy of the Hours, especially using such resources as the monthly *Magnificat* (which contains the essential prayers of the LOH for the major hours of each day).[16] It is a beautiful way for your family to tap into the traditions of the Church. There is a sense of awe and wonder that is brought forth when explaining to your children that these prayers have been prayed by Christians for centuries. Perhaps just start with morning, evening, or night prayer and increase as you see fit.[17]

THE DOMESTIC CHURCH AND
THE COMMUNION OF SAINTS

The mystical body of Christ is united but is threefold: the Church Militant (those of us here on earth still battling for holiness), the Church Suffering (the poor souls in purgatory), and the Church Triumphant (those who are enjoying eternal bliss with God in heaven). We have much to be thankful for as the body of Christ works together through prayer for one another. The communion of saints—the Church Triumphant—is a precious gift from which we may seek wisdom, inspiration, and intercession.

No matter our state in life or the struggles we face, there is a saint we can call on to intercede for us, someone who has already fought the good fight and finished the race (see 2 Timothy 4:7–8). Celebrating these saints in our homes can strengthen our domestic church and give us an opportunity to share their heroic stories with our children. There are many creative ways you can celebrate these saints: making a special cake or cookies, watching a movie about the life of the saint, coloring pages for children, singing songs, or praying together for their intercession.

For example, one way to celebrate the feast of St. Joseph the Worker is to purchase a small toolbox for each child in your family. Every year on the first of May, give a new tool and teach each how to use it. Explain how St. Joseph would have taught Jesus the function and purpose of each tool and the importance of taking pride in finishing the work that has been started. As your children grow older, they will have not only a better understanding of St. Joseph and the role he can play in their life but also a full set of quality tools in their toolbox.

The feast of All Saints' Day is a great opportunity to promote the communion of saints. Invite Catholic family friends over for dinner, encouraging all children to dress up as their favorite saint. As they put on their costume, this is a great opportunity to teach how the saint lived a heroic, virtuous life. Make sure to emphasize the different virtues the saints displayed throughout their lives. Once they are dressed, have them go outside and process from one end of the yard to the other. The leader of the group can be carrying a crucifix, and each child can hold a candle to show they have the light of Christ. Bonus points if you play "When the Saints Go Marching In." This does not have to be a lot of additional work for parents.[18]

So what is the point of all of this? Does living liturgically boil down to just some fun Catholic activities and more reasons to have parties? Not at all. Bringing the liturgical experience into your home means providing physical reminders of spiritual realities. These realities can be easily experienced within our parish church every Sunday. But what about the rest of the week? Bringing the liturgy to the daily life of our homes will invigorate everyone in our families to live more deeply for Christ! And yes, it also gives us more reasons to celebrate the intricate and beautiful life of the Church. And to eat cake.

If you are wondering where to start, just look at a Church calendar and simply choose a day. Pick a beloved saint, the anniversary of your baptism, or any Sunday, for that matter. Next, decide how you want your domestic church to participate and celebrate in unison with the life of the greater Church. Planning well, be it simple or extravagant, will help the celebration be a success. A great rule of thumb is to have a great group of people, delicious food, and a new (or old) activity in which to participate. Don't forget that attending Holy Mass is always a great way to celebrate any occasion!

The journey to developing a sense of liturgy in the home may take some time. Like St. Thérèse of Lisieux, if we can only humble ourselves and walk along the "Little Way," one foot after the other, how pleasing would each step be to Christ? Only God knows what lies ahead of us during this tumultuous time, but let us allow peace to envelop us by bringing the liturgy closer to our hearts and home.

All Saints' Day Prayer

Father, all-powerful and ever-living God, today we rejoice in the holy men and women of every time and place. May their prayers bring us your forgiveness and love. We ask this through our Lord Jesus Christ, your Son, who lives and reigns with you and the Holy Spirit, God, for ever and ever.

6

THE LANGUAGE OF THE DOMESTIC CHURCH

Is there a more beautiful sound than hearing little children singing or praying at Mass? When those sounds echo in the Church, does it not give all a rush of joy and hope?

As parents, it is our duty to teach our children the appropriate responses and cadence within the Eucharistic Liturgy. If the Eucharist is the "source and summit of the Christian life" (CCC 1324)—and if we truly believe this— then it is an act of justice to God that we honor him the way the Church has asked. The Liturgy is the source of our spiritual life, from which grace flows. Since grace builds on nature, it is important that we, as a family but more broadly as the mystical body of Christ, cooperate in this liturgical action so that it produces its fruits in our lives.

By observing our example, our children will learn how to properly participate in the Holy Sacrifice of the Mass. For example, they will see us bless ourselves with holy water as we enter the church and will learn to do the same. Likewise, they will see us genuflect, paying honor to our Lord in the tabernacle, as we enter and leave the pew and will mimic our actions. It doesn't take long before our children know when to sit, stand, or kneel in the liturgy. In the Eucharistic Liturgy, we all know our lines and the appropriate responses, but there are a number of lines and responses we need to learn in the "domestic liturgy."

SPEAKING THE LANGUAGE OF VIRTUES

As a father, watching your sons play football is such a joy. Eavesdropping on their conversations as they decide which team they will be, who gets the ball first, if they plan to go for it on fourth down, and what routes they plan to run all before a single, "Down, set, hut!" If boys want to be football players when they grow up, they will have a desire to study the game and the meaning of a crossing route, the silent count, or "Cover 2" defense. Learning the strategies and philosophy of football will better prepare them for possible Friday night games under the stadium lights.

If you want to be a football player, you need first to learn the language of football. Similarly, if we want to be virtuous, we need to use the "language of virtue"—that is, we must speak virtuously. As a holy priest once said, "If you want your children to be just, kind, and patient, you should use the words 'just,' 'kind,' and 'patient.' The words become the goal." This quite literally means saying the actual words you want them to become familiar with. Our children are listening, and they will take each word you say to connect with the world around them. Continuing with the football analogy, there is an "offensive game plan" and a "defensive game plan" when promoting the use of virtuous words in the home. (Of course, we should always avoid using "offensive" words!)

When we go on "offense" and use virtuous words and seek to act virtuously, our children will learn how to speak and act virtuously. As the *Catechism* states, we come to learn that "human virtues are firm attitudes, stable dispositions, habitual perfections of intellect and will that govern our actions, order our passions, and guide our conduct according to reason and faith" (CCC 1804). These habitual good actions build virtue, and "virtue is the utmost of what a man can be; it is the realization of the human capacity for being."

As every parent knows, while living virtuously and encouraging our children to do the same is essential, we need a "defensive game plan" as well. In charity, we must correct bad speech and behavior and strategically defend our children from vice. Even good children can do bad things. When correcting bad behavior, we need to focus on the action rather than the child. Of course, correcting a child's bad behavior isn't enough; we must steer them in the right direction to desire the virtuous acts. Children need to know what the end goal is and how to win. And if our goal is to "run in such a way that you may win," as St. Paul teaches us, then we must not merely teach what not to do but also what to do so they might win even when we are not present.

TONE OF LANGUAGE

During a speaker series held by St. Michael Catholic Radio in Tulsa, Oklahoma, Catholic speaker and apologist Tim Staples gave an off-the-cuff glimpse into a practice in his own household. With fatherly guidance, he taught his family to make a slight bow of the head any time they would hear the name of Jesus. Likewise, any time they would speak the name of Jesus, it must always be done in a reverent, almost prayerful tone.

This is a great way to bring practices from the Eucharistic Liturgy into your domestic church. As the *General Instruction of the Roman Missal* states, "A bow of the head is made when the three Divine Persons are named together and at the names of Jesus, of the Blessed Virgin Mary, and of the Saint in whose honor Mass is being celebrated."[19] The words we use have meaning, but the way we communicate these words should reflect our interior disposition.

Teaching our children to joyfully serve each other in the home can start with a simple, "Yes, sir (ma'am)" or "I would be happy to." By encouraging the use of language that reflects gratitude and a willingness to help, we can form habits of loving our neighbor as ourselves. There are many other phrases we must learn to say often within the home, such as, "I love you," "I'm sorry," "Thank you for dinner," and "How was your day?" Our children will learn if we truly mean these words by how we say them. Children come to know, understand, and appreciate the love of God through their parents, so we, as parents, need to show them the charity within our words and actions.

RESPECT FOR OTHERS

Sunday night with extended family gathered around a well-decorated dinner table for a special event or celebration is one of our fondest childhood memories. Grandparents, aunts and uncles, and cousins gathered with Mom and Dad and siblings to share not just a meal but our lives with one another. The transition from us all being silent before saying grace quickly burst into multiple conversations happening around the table. Before the meal was over, our grandparents would address the family to give insightful commentary on something that was happening within the family or a current event. We had been taught that when Grandma and Grandpa were speaking, we all would respectfully be quiet and listen attentively. They had a valued level of perspective and experience that was irreplaceable and unobtainable in the current state of our lives.

Piety—which comes from the Latin *pietas*, meaning "dutiful" or "devout"—is the virtue by which an individual has a duty to honor God, parents, and country. But because piety is not only a virtue but also a gift of the Holy Spirit, St. Thomas Aquinas and other theologians insisted that piety belonged in a special category. We owe a debt of gratitude to those in our lives who give us a holy example of how to live out the Christian virtues. The gift of the Holy Spirit completes and perfects those virtues.[20]

Our children will inevitably have difficulties in their lives. We cannot stop that from happening, as we know the way of the Christian life is carrying the Cross. What we can do is instill in our children respect for their elders and a desire to seek their guidance. If they don't seek counsel from the people who truly love them, like grandparents and parents, they will seek it from other places. Providing opportunities for families to gather together and seek wisdom from one another is vital for a healthy and holy upbringing.

As Archbishop Fulton J. Sheen once said, "If it be true that the world has lost its respect for authority, it is only because it lost it first in the home."[21] The words and actions we choose within the domestic church get passed on from generation to generation. It starts in the home. And in the home, it starts with the words we choose. St. Paul tells us, "Faith comes from what is heard, and what is heard comes by the preaching of Christ" (Romans 10:17).

Prayer for the Day's Work at Home

God, be in my head, and in my understanding;

God, be in my eyes, and in my looking;

God, be in my mouth, and in my speaking;

God, be in my heart, and in my thinking;

God, be at my end, and at my departing.

7

THE HOME OF THE DOMESTIC CHURCH

Our house is a physical manifestation of the process of sanctification. It is not holy in the same way as a church altar or tabernacle but in a natural, practical way. The words *sacred*, *sacrament*, and *sacrifice* all come from the Latin root word *sanctus*, which means "holy" or "set apart." Something is considered holy when it is removed from common use and "set apart" exclusively for the service of God. On a natural level, this is exactly why we build houses—to take a piece of earth and "set it apart" from the rest of the world exclusively in the service of a domestic church and the rites that take place within.

There is nothing more common for a house than to have walls. Think about how different your house would be if it did not have any interior or exterior walls. Could you even still call it a house? The idea of living in a two-story gazebo is certainly a comical one, but imagine how dysfunctional life would be trying to accommodate such an arrangement: No way to keep the place warm in the winter and having to wait till midnight to shower so as not to scandalize the neighbors, not to mention trying to keep the raccoons out of your kitchen at night and the fact that the whole place would flood every time it rained. Every step in the domestic liturgy would be devastated.

Without walls, nothing is established. The walls of the home serve to safeguard and dignify all that takes place within them. They establish the boundaries of where we work, and where we rest; where we cook, and where we feast. The walls show us how important dining together is by setting apart a room where dining is the only thing we do there, in order to give dining the honor it deserves. Now, of course, not all houses are created equal. A well-ordered house is one that honors the dignity of ordinary life by setting apart a place for ordinary, everyday undertakings.

But what about the rooms themselves? What do we find when we look at them individually? We find service and celebration, the cross and heaven. The ceremonies of each room guide us in their own way toward the same mantra of love—namely, that we lay down our lives for others.

BEDROOM

Have you ever considered how well named each room of the house is? A living room is not just for sitting but for *living*; the dining room isn't just for eating food but for *dining*; and a bedroom is not just for sleeping. Of all the rooms in the house, a bedroom is the most exclusive. As a guest in someone's home, it is understood that you do not have automatic permission to casually stroll into the master bedroom the way you would, say, the living or dining rooms. While your host might invite you into the house and welcome you to the living room, dining room, and family room, there is no implied permission for you to roam freely—and certainly not to enter the bedrooms. A separate invitation is necessary.

In the bedroom we find the extremes of life. It is where life begins and where it ends, where we encounter our greatest joys and our greatest sorrows. It is the consummation of the vows taken at the altar (the bed itself is an altar) and where we find rest from a hard day's work done in service of those vows. Ultimately, the bedroom is so holy because it represents our life's vocation. I lay down my life for you so much that I freely choose to set myself apart from all others in order that I might love you alone with all my power to do so.

KITCHEN

The kitchen is one of the most important rooms in the house. If the kitchen doesn't function properly, chaos will command the home. The kitchen is also the servant of the household because nothing we do in the kitchen is *for* the kitchen. Whether you are preparing a meal or cleaning up after one, the activities of the kitchen are always ordered toward another. The kitchen does all the hard work, and the dining room gets all the glory, and this is its beauty. It is here that we learn that a life in service to others is one filled with joy and chocolate cake. I lay down my life for yours, now please pass the cake.

DINING ROOM (or Wherever the Family Shares a Meal)

On a strictly natural level, most of the household is ordered toward the dinner table. We have strong walls and a safe place to sleep so that we can ensure our ability to eat three times a day. However, when we share a meal, we are not just satisfying a biological necessity, we are celebrating the lives of everyone present and some who are not.

By the time the family sits down at the dinner table, its "mantra of love" ("I lay down my life for yours") has played itself out many times. As we gather around the table, we "consummate" (consume) the life of another that has been laid down for us. Whether it is the life of a cow, chicken, fish, or vegetable, the hard work of the farmer or the cook, we give glory to this mantra of love in hopeful anticipation of one day sitting down together at the eternal banquet of heaven.

Since Adam and Eve took the forbidden fruit from the tree and fell, Jesus allowed himself to be hung on a tree and become our food, saying, in effect, "I lay down my life for yours, now come and be satisfied"—which we do when we receive Our Lord in the Eucharist. In a small way, every time we sit down at the table together in our domestic church, we image the communion we have with Christ and the universal Church. With this in mind, it is easy to see why we insist that the fork is in just the right place, that the candles are lit, and impose an etiquette upon ourselves. This is the height of the domestic liturgy. It may seem silly and superfluous to busy ourselves with charger plates and salad forks, but these things endow an elegance and decorum to that which deserves our honor—namely, a life laid down that we might live.

LIVING ROOM

Of all the rooms in the house, the living room is unique because it is difficult to say exactly what its purpose is. It is not dedicated to one essential function of family life. Rather, it is a catch-all for everything that does not have a specific place somewhere else. As Thomas Howard says in his book *Hallowed Be This House*, "The idea in living rooms down through the centuries has been that there is an entity 'the family,' such that their mere being together is a good thing and that an ordinary house will have space provided for that mere being together."[22]

The living room is where we attend the school of charity because there we must learn to govern ourselves. In contrast, the dining room (or dinner table) has specific rules: we each sit in a certain spot, we say grace before meals, we speak in certain ways (e.g., asking another to pass the gravy), we do not discuss certain unpleasant topics (e.g., things that would ruin the appetite), and we stay until everyone has finished, all the while doing a specific thing—eating. The dining room has a very concrete script that children and adults alike learn to follow.

In the living room, though, it is more of a ceremonial "free-for-all." This particular space in our domestic church forces us to take what we have learned about how to love one another and put it into practice. When children compromise on what book mom is going to read or learn to share their toys, in a small way, they are saying to one another, "I lay down my life for yours." Finally, the living room is the only room in the house not ordered toward a biological necessity. It is only after the meals have been eaten and the work has been completed that we have time to sit and just be together. The living room is ordered not toward the body but the *person*. This room professes that we are good, in and of ourselves, as children of God;

it has been set apart for us to simply *be* with one another as a domestic church, apart from any other task or activity.

AT HOME WITH JESUS

Jesus comes to us in both exceptional and ordinary ways—in the Eucharist and at the dinner table, respectively. He is present in our domestic churches just as he was present in Joseph and Mary's domestic church two thousand years ago. May every room of our house be filled with the love and mercy of Christ—and may we glorify him in all of our ordinary everyday ways.

Here are some practical suggestions for the home of your domestic church:

- Keep a clean, tidy house to show respect for the family.

- Make sure each child knows how to do chores—e.g., pick up toys and other possessions; do laundry, fold, and put away their clothes; run the vacuum; sweep the floors; dust the furniture; take out the trash; etc.

- Use proper manners always, particularly during meals.

- As a parent, set an example of leisure by completing all your work or obligations before you engage in leisure, recreation, or rest.

- Do things together in the family room— as a family.

Psalm 84

How lovely is your dwelling place,
   O LORD of hosts!
My soul longs, yes, faints
   for the courts of the LORD;
my heart and flesh sing for joy
   to the living God.

Even the sparrow finds a home,
   and the swallow a nest for herself,
   where she may lay her young,
at your altars, O LORD of hosts,
   my King and my God.
Blessed are those who dwell in your house,
   ever singing your praise!

Blessed are the men whose strength is in you,
   in whose heart are the highways to Zion.
As they go through the valley of Baca
   they make it a place of springs;
   the early rain also covers it with pools.
They go from strength to strength;
   the God of gods will be seen in Zion.

O LORD God of hosts, hear my prayer;
  give ear, O God of Jacob!
Behold our shield, O God;
  look upon the face of your anointed!

For a day in your courts is better
  than a thousand elsewhere.
I would rather be a doorkeeper in the house of my God
  than dwell in the tents of wickedness.
For the LORD God is a sun and shield;
  he bestows favor and honor.
No good thing does the LORD withhold
  from those who walk uprightly.
O LORD of hosts,
  blessed is the man who trusts in you!

8

HOLY LEISURE IN THE DOMESTIC CHURCH

In a world full of politics, tribalism, economic uncertainties, health concerns, and relativism, is now really the time to be talking about leisure? Jobs require more time in the office (even if this is "virtual"), sports programs demand more time on the practice fields, and secular holidays invade our calendars unapologetically. Our "to-do" list is undoubtedly growing at a pace that will require every ounce of our energy if we are to realistically attempt to cross off the endless bullet points. These duties are indeed important; they should not be neglected or taken lightly. Nonetheless, with all these tasks at hand, now would actually be a very appropriate time to make the case for leisure.

In the first chapter of Aristotle's *Metaphysics*, we learn that a principal foundation of Western culture is leisure: "We work so we can have leisure." The end of work, then, is leisure. We work so that we may rest. We do not rest so that we may work. Aristotle came to this rightful conclusion without the benefit of divine revelation but by reason alone. St. John Paul II expands on this idea, making the critical assertion that work is made for man, not man for work.[23]

From the beginning, man has been called to work to earn a living, contribute to the sciences, and elevate unceasingly the "cultural and moral level of the society within which we live."[24] Cooperating with God's grace and working to grow the kingdom in this life prepares us for the eternal rest we will have in the next. What do we say about those who have passed away? "Eternal *rest* grant unto him, O Lord, and let perpetual light shine upon him." Why do we say this? It is because we have been made for this rest. We are made to rest in Christ. As the author of the letter to the Hebrews says, "Therefore, while the promise of entering his rest remains, let us fear lest any of you be judged to have failed to reach it" (Hebrews 4:1).

So if the end of this life is so that we may rest in God, shouldn't we look to see if we are rightly preparing ourselves? Resting in Christ in this life comes from a consistent and courageous prayer life. Forming a relationship with Christ while on earth prepares us for eternal life as we will join all the choirs of angels in praising the Triune God. This rest, or leisure, is for its own sake; namely, for the love of God and giving God the Father the justice that is due to him. Although this rest can be restorative, and often times it is, the primary purpose is not for the sake of this restoration, but for the sake of its own end.

Each night our family follows a routine to prepare for bed, and it always concludes with prayer together. These habitual actions create a feeling of comfort and give the children the opportunity for a good night's rest. However, we do not pray together as a family so that our children sleep better; we pray together as a family because we desire to submit our wills to the Father's will and develop a personal relationship with our Lord. The kids sleeping better is a secondary benefit, and a big one at that, but it's not the goal. If leisure is the goal, we must take a step back and reflect on whether we are working to cultivate that goal. Work is most certainly important and meaningful. It provides practical needs, contributes to the common good, and serves some other purpose which is its essential characteristic.

In his book *Leisure: The Basis of Culture*, Josef Pieper points out that there are not only societal pressures but also personal pressures, on the "overvaluation of work."[25] All too often we think being busy means being productive, and if we aren't busy, then we are missing the opportunities to reap the benefits to provide for our family. Pieper labels

work in a threefold sense: first, the activity of work;
second, the exertion, effort, and drudgery of work; and last
but certainly not least, the social usefulness or utilitarian
purpose of work. As Pieper writes, "This specifically is the
three-faced demon everyone has to deal with when setting
out to defend leisure."[26] So let's take a look at how we, as
a family, can defend the end goal and participate in this
concept that the Fathers of the Church often referred to as
otium sanctum, or "holy leisure."

THE FIGHT AGAINST ACTIVITY

Ah, sweet, sweet, silence. As Cardinal Robert Sarah so
eloquently states, "When we retreat from the noise of the
world in silence, we gain a new perspective on the world.
To retreat into silence is to come to know ourselves, to
know our dignity."[27]

Adam and Haylee: After eight p.m., we (finally)
experience silence in our home. The children have been
tucked away in bed, the household duties have been
completed, and we have sat down to relax for the first
time in ... well, we forget how long because we are parents
of young children. However, on an ideal day, our family
attempts to have all-important "quiet times," where we
engage in a silent activity for a certain amount of time.
Sometimes these last ten minutes, other times an hour.

This simple task, which is meaningful in itself, allows our children to use their mental and physical capacity in a way that is different from any other. It cultivates in them an attitude of receptive openness and attentive silence that counterbalances the concentrated exertion needed to complete a school assignment earlier in the day. One of our children enjoys some quiet reading time, another likes to build with blocks, and another likes to silently color. There is a beauty in their autonomy to choose how they spend this special time, where they can focus solely on something they enjoy for its own sake.

As St. John of the Cross says, "It is ... much better to impose silence on the faculties and to cause them to be still, so that God may speak."[28] There are certain times when they will need to be quiet, and strengthening this skill will build a sense of reverence for that unique occasion. Our children won't learn to be silent *during* Mass; they must first learn to be silent at home and then apply this skill in church. Sunday Mass is what the family must build upon for the coming week. It must be at the forefront of what we do and who we are. As John Senior said, "What is Christian culture? It is essentially the Mass."[29]

THE FIGHT AGAINST DRUDGERY

In a Christian home, it is important to strive to make Sundays look and feel different from every other day of the week.

We should make sure we and our children are dressed appropriately for Mass—that is, in a way that honors our Lord in his Eucharistic presence. Men artfully forming their necktie into the perfect knot, women choosing a beautiful and modest dress, and the children ... well, if your children are like ours, it is a huge success if everyone is leaving the house with shoes on the correct feet!

We put on our "Sunday best" because Sunday is a solemn day. It is the feast of the sacrificial Lamb of God. It is the day Catholics throughout the world come together to participate in Christ's Passover, the day that "fulfills the spiritual truth of the Jewish Sabbath and announces man's eternal rest in God" (CCC 2175). Divine worship is the "most festive festival" possible to celebrate, as Joseph Pieper states.[30] But putting on our "Sunday best" does not stop with what we are wearing when we go to Mass.

Sunday brings out the beauty of leisure in a way that should stop us in our tracks and gently ease us away from the "busyness" and noise of our everyday lives. It is a day to feast with our family and friends, to avoid unnecessary trips to stores or restaurants, to forgo household responsibilities, and to turn off exterior distractions—to unplug from being mindlessly glued to our devices. It is a day to celebrate, free from our everyday exertion.

Creating a habit of making Sunday a special day must be intentional. After all, we are easily distracted, especially in our technology-driven age. As St. Thomas Aquinas says, "The human mind is unable to remain aloft for long on account of the weakness of nature because human weakness weighs down the soul to the level of inferior things: and hence it is that when, while praying, the mind ascends to God by contemplation, of a sudden it wanders off through weakness."[31] To foster a spirit of prayer and contemplation on Sunday, we must plan our week accordingly and get everything done on the preceding days.

THE FIGHT AGAINST SOCIAL USEFULNESS

Adam and Haylee: As a family, there are times when we need to come together to do certain tasks. All of us work constantly to keep our homes clean and orderly. (As every family knows, this is a perpetual battle.) Every week, each member of the family is responsible for completing the chores assigned to him or her. As each child matures, more responsibility is given to him or her based on ability. When our sons become old enough, or think they have become old enough, to mow the yard, we show them the proper way to do so and then let them take a crack at it. It takes mighty effort and fortitude for a seven-year-old to navigate a mower around the yard. Eventually, he will tire and need a much-deserved break. His break may include going inside for lunch, relaxing on the patio chair outside, or even playing in a quick pickup game of football with his siblings. This break, however, is not the same as leisure time. The break, regardless of the length, is designed for relaxation in anticipation of more work.

Leisure is something entirely different. "Leisure," as Pieper puts it, "is not to assure that we may function smoothly but rather to assure that we, embedded in our social function, are enabled to remain fully human."[32] This is why it is important as parents to allow our children to stargaze, read a novel, explore nature, sing a song, or recite poetry. These activities allow for contemplation, creativity, celebration, and wonder—and are focused on their own significance and not for other utilitarian purposes. As John Senior rightly points out, "All architecture, art, political and social forms, economics, the way people live and feel and think, music, literature—all these things when they are right, are ways of fostering and protecting the Holy Sacrifice of the Mass."[33] The world tells us that too much is never enough and that we are made to be relentlessly working, ultimately for the goal of accumulating material wealth. As Christians, though, we can contemplate and celebrate that we are made in God's image and likeness, knowing that regardless of what the world offers us, our hearts will be restless until they rest in him.

It was a sense of wonder, stillness, and receptivity that brought the ancient Greeks out of a world of materialism and to conclude that we work so that we may leisure. It is no surprise that today's attacks on silence, the sacred, and the arts force us to fight this same battle against materialism. As a Christian family, our goal is heaven. We can only achieve this goal by living a sacramental life, cooperating with God's grace, and keeping our eyes fixed on eternal life, so that one day we may hear the words, "Well done, good and faithful servant"—and have true leisure by resting in him.

The Song of the Three Young Men in Daniel 3

Blessed are you, O Lord, God of our fathers,
   and to be praised and highly exalted for ever;
And blessed is your glorious, holy name
   and to be highly praised and highly exalted for ever.

9

SERVICE IN THE DOMESTIC CHURCH

Building a domestic church, brick by brick, is an intentional, selfless labor of love. It is a daily decision to serve others instead of serving yourself. Each brick must carefully be placed to create a loving and stable home, allowing each member of the family to fulfill their baptismal duty to evangelize all the nations. As St. John Paul II states, "As the family goes, so goes the nation, and so goes the whole world in which we live."[34]

As parents, we must bear witness to this responsibility first by creating a home where tenderness, forgiveness, respect, fidelity, and disinterested service are the rule (see CCC 2223). Most of these qualities are self-evident and obvious, but the last one may seem surprising. Disinterested service, or holy indifference, helps one cultivate God's kingdom in a home by choosing the good of the other rather than one's own. Developing this selfless attitude of service will likely produce a noble mosaic of virtues, which imitate and reflect God's own goodness. Serving others in our domestic church disinterestedly by setting aside our own personal desires allows us to love each member of our family sacrificially, reflecting the sacrificial love of Jesus. And this is true love, as St. Thomas Aquinas states. As Jesus tells us, "If you lend to those from whom you hope to receive, what credit is that to you? Even sinners lend to sinners, to receive as much again" (Luke 6:34).

SPOUSE TO SPOUSE

The love between spouses sets the tone for every other relationship within the home. If we want to love one another well, then we must first place ourselves in the obedient service of our vocation. In his first letter to the Corinthians, St. Paul speaks about the disinterested service in which love rules: "Love is patient and kind. ... Love does not insist on its own way" (1 Corinthians 13:4–5). Love is a choice, as any successful marriage can attest. Identify your spouse's needs in order to love him or her in the best way; don't be afraid to ask, "My love, how can I serve you better today?" Experience shows that you might be surprised by his or her response! In doing so, you are living out your vocation while simultaneously growing closer to your beloved by knowing him or her better.

To serve in an authentically disinterested way, we must cultivate a humble heart. This selfless loving must become ingrained in the everyday interactions between husband and wife if it is to truly become part of the family culture. Moms and dads must lead by example. The challenges will be manifold, but continually putting the other's needs first, being grateful, being helpful, and anticipating the needs of the other will help curb the temptation to keep track of who is "earning the most brownie points."

Not everyone gives and receives love in the same way. Words of affirmation, physical touch, receiving gifts, quality time, and acts of service are what Gary Chapman calls the five love languages.[35] Everyone has a "love language" in which he or she prefers to give and receive expressions of love. Chances are good that the way you prefer to express love might not be the language that makes your spouse feel loved the most. Maybe you are a gift-giving kind of guy, but nothing makes your wife feel more cared for than when you go out of your way to empty the dishwasher for her. If you don't know already, find out your spouse's love language and begin to speak it.

PARENT TO CHILD

The first and essential gift a parent gives to their children is the gift of life. Christ brings forth children through his goodness, and we, as parents, have the responsibility of selfless service to his perfect creation. "Parents must regard their children as children of God and respect them as human persons. Showing themselves obedient to the will of the Father in heaven, they educate their children to fulfill God's law" (CCC 2222). Being obedient to the will of the Father means detaching ourselves from our own will, as difficult as this is at times.

While every family has unique qualities, the fundamental objective must be to lead each other to the ultimate destination, the kingdom of heaven. Whether you're a family of four with a single source of income, a family of eight with both parents working outside of the home, empty-nesters, parents of children with special needs, or whatever the case, the target is eternal life. As most parents know, serving children with a loving heart isn't always a walk in the park. Rarely will a child resound with celebratory trumpets blaring in your honor after you have prepared the third meal of the day or with a round of applause for successfully fixing the plumbing under the kitchen sink. It can undoubtedly be a thankless job. However, always be reminded that you have enabled your children, by the very gift of their life, to grow in wisdom and grace. They will learn the fulfillment of serving others by the way you serve them.

CHILD TO PARENT

When all members of the family are focused on achieving a goal together, it is a beautiful sight to behold. Each member knows the importance of carrying out his or her duty for the greater good of the family.

Adam and Haylee: Recently, we engaged in some outdoor chores. The leaves needed to be raked, the wood needed to be split, the grass needed to be cut, and the garden needed to be tended. We told our children that they all needed to get this work done for Mom so she could focus on homeschooling during the week. One was assigned raking, another mowing the lawn, while Adam started preparing to split the wood. We watched the kids independently work hard for their mother and for the greater good of the family. In between splitting wood, he noticed the boys were moving a little slower than earlier and considered calling for a break. As Adam was setting the ax down, out walked our young daughter beaming with excitement and holding a cup full of ice-cold water for Dad and the boys. Adam thanked her for the water, and she joyfully went running back into the house, proud that she was able to help. Each member of the family is called to serve, in his or her own way, for the common good of the family, and this includes the children, even young children, serving their parents. Children thrive on responsibility, and if we don't give them opportunities to serve others, we are doing them a disservice and not fulfilling our duty as parents to prepare them for the world. For we, as parents, are called to help establish in them a servant's heart for the vulnerable, elderly, sick, disabled, and poor. Where will they learn to serve others well if they do not start in their home?

SIBLING TO SIBLING

Teaching your children to serve one another will have everlasting effects. Think of the different skills it takes to serve someone else well. One must practice selflessness, compassion, gratitude, humility, empathy, and attentiveness. Among the siblings is where the concept of disinterested service can be most difficult.

The seed of service, sown well, will produce the mosaic of virtues that are needed to enter the kingdom of God. In turn, these virtues will bear fruit. Kindness is certainly the current "buzzword," yet how much more beneficial is service. When an older sibling can fraternally correct or even help to keep a younger sibling safe, there is not a natural reward to which the former can look forward. This act of selflessness for the other should not go unnoticed or unpraised. Plus, it can really cut down on the tattling!

David and Pamela: Some of our children participate in Catechesis of the Good Shepherd, a Montessori-based religious formation. One of the benefits we have seen is the willingness on the part of our children to assist with chores and demonstrate specific skills to other siblings. They have learned the value of doing something well for someone who is in need, especially if you excel in one area when your sibling does not. Even the toddler in the family will find enjoyment in the humble service of taking debris from the older child's craft to the garbage can. Having a sense of responsibility and duty to one another is paramount in developing a servant's heart.

Prayer of St. Ignatius of Loyola

*Eternal Lord of all things, I make my oblation
with your favor and help, in presence of your
infinite goodness and in presence of your glorious
Mother and of all the saints of the heavenly court;
that I want and desire, and it is my deliberate
determination, if only it be your greater service and
praise, to imitate you in bearing all injuries and all
abuse and all poverty of spirit, and actual poverty,
too, if your most Holy Majesty wants to choose and
receive me to such life and state.*

10

HOSPITALITY IN THE DOMESTIC CHURCH

"God created man in his own image, in the image of God he created him; male and female he created them" (Genesis 1:27). Man is made in the image of his Creator *for* his Creator. In other words, God is an outpouring of love, and he created us out of this love so that we too might be an outpouring of love. The very first instruction God gives to humanity is to "be fruitful and multiply, and fill the earth and subdue it" (Genesis 1:28). Despite the whole forbidden fruit episode when their disobedience brought sin and death into the world, lost their original innocence, realized they were naked, were kicked out of paradise, and brought suffering and toil upon their descendants, this is exactly what Adam and Eve did! Sinners though they were, their love for one another, by the blessing of God, has cascaded down through the centuries from generation to generation right down to you and me.

If humanity is made in God's image in an outpouring of love, then the domestic church is likewise called to be an outpouring of love. The domestic church is the school of charity where we first learn to love those closest to us—as spouses, fathers, mothers, siblings—then, like the concentric circles of the ripple in a pond, we learn to love those outside our immediate family, such as our friends, neighbors, and fellow parishioners. This ripple of love then spreads further outward into learned charity toward the stranger. But how do we love those outside of our domestic church? Through *hospitality*.

Hospitality is the habitual disposition to invite others to share in the life and love of one's own family. This is one thing that makes hospitality unique among the virtues; it is not so much the person who exercises the virtue as it is the household. This is true even for the single person, although it is less obvious. The household is the mediator through which hospitality is administered.

David: For example, let's say that Adam invited you over for some of his famous jalapeno-cream-cheese-filled-bacon-wrapped-smoked pork loin. The next day, aside from still salivating over your previous night's meal, when you were describing the evening to some of your friends, you probably wouldn't say, "Adam had me over for dinner last night, oh, and his wife and kids were there, too."

You would say something like, "The Minihan clan had me over for dinner last night. They are such a nice family." The virtue of hospitality is a team effort involving every member of the family, each participating as they are able.

Hospitality is one of the primary forces that builds a community, and it is something that every domestic church should be striving for. It is true that not everyone is called to the same kind or degree of hospitality, but the domestic church, by its nature, is oriented outward, and hospitality is the virtue by which the domestic church interacts with the world. Through hospitality we build new friendships and strengthen old ones; neighbors become family friends, and friends become brothers. It is often in these moments when the most natural and effective evangelization takes place.

Hospitality is something that comes naturally to the domestic church when order is present in the home. When there is cooperation between husband and wife, when the children know how to behave respectfully (especially at the table), and when the house is in a general state of cleanliness, then putting hospitality into practice seems to come with ease and joy. By contrast, if the children are constantly fighting and there is disunity between the spouses, then it is almost impossible to avoid the whole thing turning into a huge blood bath, and not the good kind either, like we see Jesus doing in Revelation 7:14.

What should be a time of happiness and joy turns into awkwardness for your guests and an embarrassing form of domestic suffering for all parties.

There is another side of hospitality that must be discussed before moving on. It is not enough to roll out the red carpet and slaughter the fattened calf to satisfy the dictates of hospitality. Hospitality is so much more than just hosting; hospitality must also be received. It is an exchange of love, a giving and receiving between specific persons. It is not like giving money to charity where you know that your money will be used in a worthy manner toward someone who needs it. There is no "someone" with hospitality; hospitality says, "This one." The virtue of hospitality welcomes the other face-to-face and says, "Come share with me the good things I have received from the Lord." Try to practice hospitality on a deserted island, and you will see what I mean. I suppose you could try to harness your inner St. Francis of Assisi and prepare a meal for the birds on the island or share your shelter with a local island mouse, but even then the birds and the mouse are the "other" to whom you are being hospitable.

The final quality of hospitality is that it is prudentially disinterested. True hospitality is not self-serving. If we are only willing to extend ourselves to the members of our community that we like or those with a good reputation, then are we really practicing the virtue of hospitality? Hospitality gives of itself because it recognizes the value and dignity of the person to whom it is being offered. As Christians, we have an obligation not to "neglect to show hospitality to strangers, for thereby some have entertained angels unawares" (Hebrews 13:2).

We have some friends who make it a point to introduce themselves to any new families they see at church on Sunday and invite them over for brunch. They always keep their Sundays free and make sure they have enough food for a new family to join them. This is a beautiful example of hospitality. (Of course, there may be situations where prayerful prudence must overshadow hospitality. We may discern that, for the good of our family, we cannot welcome certain people into our home.) By practicing hospitality, we can guide our domestic churches to become witnesses of Christ's love in the world.

Hospitality is one of the fruits of the domestic church. Just as a good tree bears good fruit (see Matthew 7:17), a domestic church with a healthy and thriving family life will be naturally hospitable. What does it take to have a healthy and thriving family life? As previously mentioned, order. It takes a home where the relationship between husband and wife is upheld as the primary relationship, where the father understands his role as head and servant, and where the mother is its heart. Order must govern the language we use, the homes we choose to buy (not all houses are created equal), and it must govern our balance between disinterested service and leisure. These things will not automatically create the virtue of hospitality (or any other virtue for that matter) as if by some law of physics, but they *will* create a fertile environment for the virtues to be cultivated in ourselves and in our children. The more virtuous the individual members of our domestic church, the more hospitable the household.

SOME CONCLUDING THOUGHTS

The saint is not the person who never falls,
but rather the one who never fails to get up
again, humbly and with a holy stubbornness.
– St. Josemaría Escrivá, Friends of God

In this book, we have shared some reflections on how to make your domestic church stronger and unite your entire family more fully with God. This is the ultimate goal of our homes—to create an environment where virtues can grow and each member can help one another draw closer to our Lord. As St. John Paul II proclaims, "Willed by God in the very act of creation, marriage and the family are interiorly ordained to fulfillment in Christ."[36]

As we go about our day, it is easy to lose ourselves in the mundane and monotonous tasks of family life. But it is in those very tasks that God's grace gives us the strength to keep growing in his love as a family. As we have seen, as fathers and mothers, we need to build our domestic church with ideas and attitudes we have received from our faith and developed over time, always open to our heavenly Father's guidance, to guide them to the true, good, and beautiful. We have an obligation to shield our children from the storm of popular culture and stand up for the love of God. We have the opportunity to raise them up in the way they should go (see Proverbs 22:6)—and help create saints for the kingdom.

Practically speaking, building "holy walls" around our domestic church takes significant and persistent effort. As we have seen, introducing the liturgy of the church through feasting and fasting throughout the year, using the liturgical calendar to show the beauty of our faith with each passing season, and celebrating the beautiful saints who have gone before us are just a few ways we can enrich our family culture. Good family culture creates good families. Good families build good communities.

The love among a family should compel each member to do his or her part in serving one another with no strings attached. As Cardinal Raymond Burke has said, "There is no greater force against evil in the world than the love of a man and woman in marriage. After the Holy Eucharist, it has a power beyond anything that we can imagine."[37] Placing the other above ourself reflects the love the Father has given us through his Son, Jesus. An "attitude of gratitude" goes a long way in the cultivation of this rule of service. Using respectful and loving language toward another shows his or her true dignity as a brother, sister, father, or mother—

as one created and loved by God. Practice carrying out your duty and role in your family with grace, with dying to yourself and living for the other, and witness the unfolding of love and comfort it brings within.

Imagine these walls in your domestic home being filled with the love and service of each unique individual. As St. John Paul II says, "To maintain a joyful family requires much from both the parents and children. Each member of the family has to become, in a special way, the servant of the others."[38] Our homes can then become a slice of heaven, here on earth, working in perfect harmony. While this won't *always* be the case, wouldn't it be breathtaking to look around at this time and see your home filled with the holy images of our heavenly family, looking down upon you in joy and jubilation? On the opposite end of the spectrum, when strain and turmoil descend, having Christ come to us through the image of his passion, in the form of a crucifix, can aid us in uniting our sufferings with his. Being intentional with the design and function of our homes can take them from ordinary to extraordinary. Look at it as an outward sign of the love of our Father, not only to those living in the home, but also to those we are hosting, figuratively saying, "We want to love you as Christ loves his Church." Again, with the increased practice of the virtues, we will be more fit to be hospitable and a witness of Christ's love. We cannot give to others what we do not have.

RECOMMENDED RESOURCES

- For some helpful insights on fasting,
  particularly husbands fasting for their wives,
  visit e5men.org.

- For some suggestions on how to "live
  liturgically," visit the *Catholic All Year* blog
  at catholicallyear.com, or read *The Catholic All
  Year Compendium* by Kendra Tierney.

- Here are some suggested online resources for
  content filtering and accountability:

    - Covenant Eyes – covenanteyes.com
    - Circle – meetcircle.com
    - Bark – bark.us

- *A Short Guide to Praying as a Family: Growing
  Together in Faith and Love Each Day* by the
  Dominican Sisters of Saint Cecilia Congregation

- *Around the Year with the von Trapp Family* by Maria Augusta von Trapp

- *Hallowed Be This House* by Thomas Howard

- *Theology of Home: Finding the Eternal in the Everyday* by Carrie Gress and Noelle Mering

- *The 5 Love Languages: The Secret to Love That Lasts* by Gary Chapman

NOTES

1. Second Vatican Council, *Lumen Gentium* (November 21, 1964), 11, emphasis added.

2. John Paul II, homily given during Mass on the Mall, Washington, DC (October 7, 1979), 5, vatican.va/.

3. Second Vatican Council, *Gaudium et Spes* (December 7, 1965), 47, vatican.va/.

4. *Gaudium et Spes*, 49.

5. Adapted from *Mother Love: A Manual for Christian Mothers* (St. Mary's, KS: Angelus Press, 2012), 312.

6. Cicero, as cited in Thomas Aquinas, *Summa Theologica*, II-II.141.4.

7. John Paul II, *Mulieris Dignitatem* (August 15, 1988), 5, vatican.va/.

8. John Paul II, 17.

9. John Paul II, 18.

10.   Thomas Olmsted, pastoral document *Complete My Joy*
      (December 8, 2018), 130.

11.   *Gaudium et Spes*, 24.

12.   Shannon Collins, "The Seven Sorrows of Homeschooling
      Mothers," *Sensus Fidelium*, November 9, 2013, YouTube
      video.

13.   Pontifical Council for Justice and Peace, *Compendium of the
      Social Doctrine of the Church* (August 15, 1998), 239.

14.   Edith Stein, "The Ethos of Women's Professions," in *Essays
      on Woman: The Collected Works of Edith Stein*, vol. 2, trans.
      Freda Mary Oben (Washington, DC: ISC Publications, 1996),
      44.

15.   Adapted from *Mother Love: A Manual for Christian Mothers*,
      231.

16.   Available at us.magnificat.net.

17.   Many resources are available to learn how to pray this
      powerful prayer, including *A Layman's Guide to the Liturgy
      of the Hours: How the Prayers of the Church Can Change
      Your Life* by Fr. Timothy Gallagher, OMV (Irondale, AL:
      EWTN Publishing, 2019).

18.   Kendra Tierney offers twenty ideas for great saint
      costumes in her post "20 Easy Saint Costumes Made
      of T-Shirts," *Catholic All Year* (blog), October 26, 2021,
      catholicallyear.com/.

19. *General Instruction of the Roman Missal* (Washington, DC: USCCB, 2011), 185, usccb.org/.

20. See Aquinas, *Summa Theologica*, II-II.101; see also CCC 1831.

21. Fulton J. Sheen, *The World's First Love: Mary, Mother of God*, 2nd ed. (San Francisco: Ignatius, 2010).

22. Thomas Howell, *Hallowed Be This House: Finding Signs of Heaven in Your Home* (San Francisco: Ignatius, 2012), 48.

23. See John Paul II, *Laborem Exercens* (September 14, 1981), 6.

24. John Paul II.

25. Joseph Pieper, *Leisure: The Basis of Culture* (San Francisco: Ignatius Press, 1963), 25.

26. Pieper.

27. Robert Sarah, address at St. Michael's Cathedral, Toronto, Ontario, March 12, 2018.

28. John of the Cross, *Ascent of Mount Carmel* (London: Burns & Oates, 1983), 221.

29. John Senior, *The Restoration of Christian Culture* (Norfolk, VA: IHS Press, 2008), 17.

30. Pieper, 65.

31. Aquinas, *Summa Theologica*, II-II.83.13.1.

32. Pieper, 40.

33. Senior, 17.

34. John Paul II, homily given in Perth, Australia (November 30, 1986), 4, vatican.va/.

35. See Gary Chapman, *The 5 Love Languages* (Chicago: Northfield Publishers, 1992).

36. John Paul II, *Familiaris Consortio* (November 22, 1981), 3, vatican.va/.

37. Interview with Cardinal Raymond Burke, *LifeSiteNews*, January 21, 2015, lifesitenews.com/.

38. John Paul II, Mass on the Mall, 5.